Don't Let Me Fall

-tel.

-tel.

Copyright © 2020 -tel.
Published by Pressing on Press
All photos are works from -tel.
All rights reserved.

ISBN-13: 978-0-9862213-3-0

First Edition
September 2020

DEDICATION

To My Dad:
Wish I could sit and talk to you just one more time.
Miss you every day.

To My Mom:
The greatest gift given to me, is you as my Mom.
I love you so much.

-tel.

CONTENTS

1   Light Fades Out   9

hand

moments

goodbye

nature's tears

one hundred-twenty times

fallin'

shhhhh!

reflection

inside, outside

underneath

sadness

drops

by

clock

claim

trapped

sit

setting

I weep alone

headstone

direction

dragonfly

lost

possiblities

-tel.

2   Darkest Hour   33

     words I

     keys, words

     into the night

     rivets

     the me I use to be

     long ago

     what's left

     fenced in

     how?

     frozen

     pen

     pencil in hand

     forward

     times up

     in the cold

     getting lost

     words II

     shelled

     below

     never bloomed

     long to bloom

3   Sunrises   57

     words III

     ready to battle

     short life

     lilacs

     go

     hidden

waves

washed up

 angels don't sleep

flight

name

through

end

beginning

habit

get started

"i love you"

it was

sunrises

love

miles and miles

4 Light Again 81

wish

more

sleep

blanket of snow

words IV

willow reflect

always

bee's flower

me, home

fall's home

strangers

lucky

in walks the unknown

-tel.

    into the past

    lilac and iris

    iris

    don't let me fall

    don't let me fall II

5 Acknowledgements

6 About the Author

LIGHT FADES OUT

HAND

You held my hand
in my first moments.
I held yours
in your last.

MOMENTS

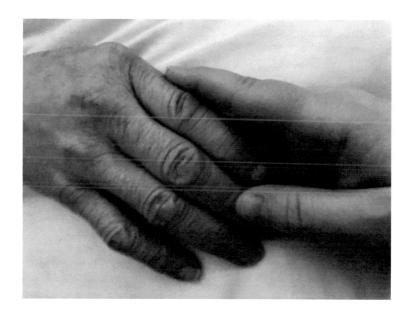

-tel.

GOODBYE

With a flood
of tears
down my cheeks,
I no longer
have you
to wipe them
away.

NATURE'S TEARS

ONE HUNDRED TWENTY TIMES

One hundred twenty times,
I whispered
your name.

One hundred twenty times,
I thought
you were beside me.

One hundred twenty times,
I learned
to live, while my heart breaks.

One hundred twenty times,
I heard
you call my name.

One hundred twenty times,
I remember
that you are now gone.

One hundred twenty times...

FALLIN'

-tel.

SHHHHH!

Hear that?
Its my tears
hitting the ground,
keeping perfect time
with the rain.

REFLECTION

INSIDE, OUTSIDE

Crying
only
on the inside.
Smiling
only
on the outside.
The rest
of the world
will never
see the
weak side
of me.

UNDERNEATH

-tel.

SADNESS

Tears collecting
in puddles,
where
your last steps
fade.

DROPS

-tel.

BY

What does it say
as I lay listening,
the clock ticks
by.

Minutes, hours, days,
longing to hear
anything else.

Trying to remember
your voice,
yet, it slips away
as the clock ticks
by.

CLOCK

CLAIM

Blackness seeps through
Its veins start to capture
every cell of your being
small wins, gives false hopes,
yet, you still cling to it,
taking the wins no matter how small,
trying to carry on.

Slowly It strikes,
not even a hint of what's to come.
Then all at once It takes hold
sucking you down, causing loss.

In the distance you hear Its chuckle,
for Its grabbed
another in Its clutches,
so you thought.
Spiraling in depths of despair
you run to get away
gone, lost, It claims another,
It claims you.

TRAPPED

SILENCE

I sit
listening
for a sound,
any sound,
but all that surrounds me
is silence.

SETTING

I WEEP ALONE

For times passed,
for lost memories,
for lost friends.
They never really knew
who I was
or
who I would become.

HEADSTONE

DIRECTION

Where does the heart guide you,
when your mind is so lost?
How does the soul sing,
when the tune has faded away?

DRAGONFLY

-tel.

DARKEST HOUR

WORDS I

Words you spit out
float above me,
like a black cloud
that never goes
Away.

KEYS, WORDS

INTO THE NIGHT

Weary bones,
joints,
limbs,
trying to rest
from the pain,
I carry throughout
the day.
Yet for the darkness
it doesn't matter
for it always
follows me
into the depths
of the night.

RIVETS

THE ME I USE TO BE

Who is that
looking back at me?
Not so long ago
I was force
to be recon with,
able to smile,
comfortable in who I was
seeing promises,
dreams to make reality.
Then FLASH,
all I was, all I could do
was gone
my world changed,
layers of unknown took its place.
Being stripped away
I no longer recognized
who I was.
The darkness consumed me,
dragged me down deep
among the depths.
A small glimmer of hope
reminding me
that I could
fight for who I was
anchoring me
so not to disappear,
to reach up
though that darkness
to be me once more.

LONG AGO

WHAT'S LEFT

Bars surround me
not of metal,
instead
they are invisible
trapped within
longing of times gone by.
For now,
for the future,
this shattered life
is all of what's left.

FENCED IN

-tel.

HOW?

How do
I make them
understand
the pain
is always
there,
even when
I'm alone.

SO COLD

-tel.

PEN

What will
become of me
the day
my hand
no longer
can hold
a pen?
How will
I write
all that
is
within,
when I can
no longer
hold
a pen.

PENCIL IN HAND

-tel.

FORWARD

"Forward,
forward," they say,
"Move forward."
but how can anyone
when every turn
leads backwards?

TIMES RUN OUT

IN THE COLD

Standing in the cold
waiting for
something to happen
but, alas
I drift off
in my own thoughts
missing the world
as it passes by.

GETTING LOST

-tel.

WORDS II

Again,
those words you spew
slash to the depths
of my soul,
til all that is left
is a
shell.

SHELLED

BELOW

Gliding just
across the surface above
the danger deep below
slightest crack
brings you close
to go through,
to be pulled down
into the depths.
You try so hard
to stay
just above.
Gliding across
reaching the safety
just in time
to see the
surface, bubble down.

ICED

-tel.

NEVER BLOOMED

How can others see
me as a strong woman,
when all I see
is a stem of a girl
who never
bloomed.

LONG TO BLOOM

-tel.

SUNRISES

WORDS III

Your words
sear the flesh,
burns so deep
I just don't know
how to win
the battle.

READY FOR BATTLE

SHORT LIFE

What a short life
lilacs have,
as if their beauty
and fragrance
is so beyond all others,
that they can't stay
too long.

LILACS

-tel.

GO

Where do I go
to hide
when all of
my hiding spots
are gone?

HIDDEN

WAVES

The waves
carry their
voice
out to sea
knowing it
needs to disappear
in order to
set you free.

WASHED UP

ANGELS DON'T SLEEP

Up where the angels don't sleep
their nightly watch keeps
the nightmares
of the world
far way,
so those
who lay awake,
can finally find
their restful peace.

FLIGHT

NAME

Your name
bounces off
the walls
as I jolt awake,
yelling for you.

THROUGH

-tel.

END

I don't know
where to begin,
but
I hope
to find
where to end.

BEGINNING

-tel.

HABIT

Creatures of habit
never really understand
the thrill seekers
of the unknown.

GET STARTED

"I LOVE YOU"

Just 3 little words
you have uttered
so many times,
but, your actions
have always shown
just how much.

REFLECTIONS

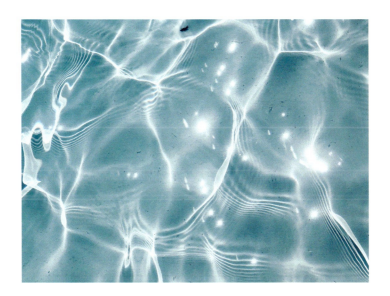

-tel.

IT WAS

There it was,
did you see it?
The light
to guide you
out of the
shadows.

SUNRISES

LOVE

Love walked
towards me.
I ask,
"Are you sure
this time?"
Love replied,
"Yes, but
are you ready?"

MILES AND MILES

-tel.

LIGHT AGAIN

WISH

You wish, you could
remember
that day
when friendship
turned
into so much
more.

MORE

SLEEP

The blanket of snow
tucks in across the land
while the wind sings
a sweet lullaby,
so the earth may
sleep again.

BLANET OF SNOW

-tel.

WORDS IV

STOP!
These words
you lash out.
I won't
let you
hold me as a
prisoner anymore.
NO!
I choose
to no longer
listen
to your
Words.

WILLOW REFLECT

-tel.

ALWAYS

On one hand
I can count
those who
have always
&
will always
be there
for me
when I need
someone
the most.

BEE'S FLOWER

ME, HOME

Your light
shines bright enough
to guide
me home.

FALL'S HOME

-tel.

STRANGERS

Met in one place,
a common interest.
Yet, would never
have known
if they hadn't
run into each other
on that
same day.

LUCKY

IN WALKS THE UNKNOWN

He wants to sit for a spell
talking of all
the events, crisis
unknown to me.

He wants to chat
of all the
knowledge, science,
and literature
unknown to me.

He wants to open
the dream box
long buried
unknown to me.

He wants to walk
explaining all that is
wondrous in the world
unknown to me.

He wants to sit a spell
watching how I
embrace all that is
unknown to me.

INTO THE PAST

LILAC AND IRIS

Hint of fragrance
lilac and iris
sweeps pass my nose
making the journey upward
you ascend there
while I am here.

We will be
back together
after the last frost melts
and the hint of
lilac and iris
sweeps pass my nose again.

IRIS

DON'T LET ME FALL

As a little girl
you were there
to always catch me.

As a teen
I wanted to do
it on my own,
even if you offered
to still catch me.

As an adult
I felt I needed
to catch myself
as well as others,
but, you were there
still to catch me.

Now that you are gone,
I long for your arms
to catch me
once more.

DON'T LET ME FALL II

ACKNOWLEDGEMENTS

To my children: R.A.A.R. my whole heart, my life, I love you more than our song(s) and ice cream.

To my siblings: Holly, Amy, Tim, Chris, we share a strong bond that will last a lifetime. Love you all so much and I enjoy every moment we spend and share together.

To Bob: Thanks for being a big part of my "entourage".

To the Archuletas: mi familia, siempre

To the Tookes: God had a reason and I am so glad He did.

To the Strykers: the best neighbors and friends anyone could ask for. 15 years and counting.

To Heather: you always understand, even when I don't. Love you and Ire so much.

To Debbie: your friendship means so much to me. Thank you for always being there.

To Annette: thank you for being there through thick and thin. I value your friendship so much.

To Lori and the boys: so many memories and joy we have shared. I always enjoy every minute we can spend together.

To Audrey: you have helped me make my dreams of being an author come true and now as a publisher. Your positive energy helps me on so many dark days.

To Janet and This Old Book: thank you for supporting this local author. You are one of the best bookstores out there.

To all my family and friends near and far: I wouldn't be me without you in every stage of my life. Love you all.

-tel.

ABOUT THE AUTHOR

-tel is the author of two other poetry collections, Ink on Paper and when willow weeps.

She is currently working on her first novel and as always her poetry.

She currently lives in a northern suburb of Chicago with her family and two cats.

Made in the USA
Columbia, SC
09 December 2024